Minding Our Manners

Saying I'm Sorry

By Kathleen Connors

Gareth Stevens
PUBLISHING

first concepts

Have you ever
taken a toy
from your sister?

Maybe you said mean things to a boy in your class.

No one is nice
all the time.

But you can try
to make up for what
you have done.

If you have hurt or
bothered someone,
you can say
you are sorry.

Think about how
the person you hurt
must feel.

Saying "I'm sorry" means you feel bad for what you did.

Saying "I'm sorry" lets others know you understand why they are hurt.

Saying "I'm sorry" is sometimes enough.

Other times, you might want to *show* that you are sorry.

N8143S

Giving a hug
or sharing a toy
is a good way
to do that!

Please visit our website, www.garethstevens.com. For a free color catalog of all our high-quality books, call toll free 1-800-542-2595 or fax 1-877-542-2596.

Library of Congress Cataloging-in-Publication Data

Connors, Kathleen.
Saying I'm sorry / Kathleen Connors.
pages cm — (Minding our manners)
Includes index.
ISBN 978-1-4824-1723-4 (pbk.)
ISBN 978-1-4824-1724-1 (6 pack)
ISBN 978-1-4824-1722-7 (library binding)
1. Apologizing—Juvenile literature. 2. Children—Conduct of life. I. Title. II. Title: Saying I am sorry.
BF575.A75C66 2015
395—dc23

2014024265

First Edition

Published in 2015 by
Gareth Stevens Publishing
111 East 14th Street, Suite 349
New York, NY 10003

Designer: Andrea Davison-Bartolotta
Editor: Kristen Rajczak

Photo credits: Cover, p. 1 David Laurens/PhotoAlto Agency RF Collections/Getty Images; p. 3 Colin Hawkins/Cultura/Getty Images; p. 5 Monkey Business Images Ltd/Monkey Business/Thinkstock; p. 7 Robert Niedring/Getty Images; p. 9 Alexey Shinkevich/Shutterstock.com; p. 11 Olimpik/Shutterstock.com; p. 13 Voyagerix/iStock/Thinkstock; p. 15 Mel Yates/The Image Bank/Getty Images; p. 17 Image Source/Getty Images; p. 19 Pressmaster/Shutterstock.com; p. 21 Randy Faris/Fuse/Thinkstock; p. 23 Nicole S. Young/iStock/Thinkstock.

Printed in the United States of America

CPSIA compliance information: Batch #CW15GS: For further information contact Gareth Stevens, New York, New York at 1-800-542-2595.